Waves of Thought

Dr. Shagufa Amber

ISBN 979-8-88935-992-0

Dedicated to my Mother (Shahina Parween),
Grandfather (Md. Shafique Akhtar),
& my loving FAMILY.

Contents

"The connection of soul is eternal
The lost gems bless us forever"

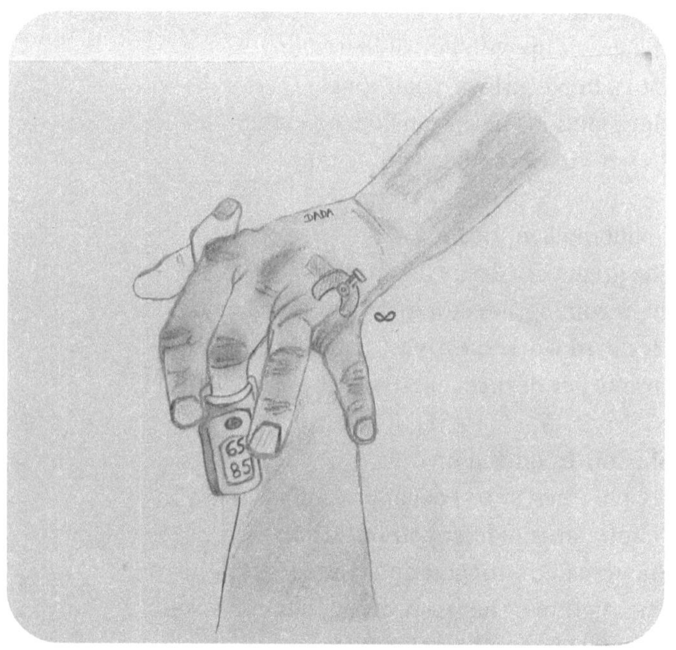

She

The dangling sperm instills life in an ova,
She suffers every pain and labor
To hear the cry of joy and pleasure.

Those vigilant eyes, capture every feature
Of this ridiculous, noteworthy theatre.
She grows up with her siblings along
Into a brave girl with hair long.
Her emotions never tangle with error,
As her virtues collide with terror.

In nut-shelled dream
She greets her desires .
Of becoming a doctor, teacher, or a martyr.
Her hard work, creativity, and titivation
Grants her desires massive expression.

She moves on and on
As a mother, sister, daughter, and friend.
Nature nurtured her soft outwardly
She remains strongest and courageous at heart.
The rhythm of her respect touches every soul
Very few reciprocate their role.
As long as 'SHE' thrives freely
Life will breathe willingly.
Embrace a girl child dear, friend.
Let mankind live till the end.

Under the Sky

Wandering under the clear sky
Embracing the ambiance with arms wide.
The soft grassy floor passes by
I continue to wander in the clear sky.

Chirping birds, and gusty wind
Swept me along in the far-field.
The budding daisy and blooming rose
Were encircled by honeybee's show.
With swings creaking to and fro
Bringing the kids more laughter and glow
Squirrel with its bushy grey tail,
Climbed up to the tail and down the nail.

Wandering under the clear sky
Was one of the best days in my life.
It connected me, with nature's bond
Discovered in me a curious vagabond.

Parents

Check my veins of reddish glow
Giving me strength and a supportive flow
How can I forget their first smile?
For my success which was theirs sometimes
They seemed to be soft yet no less harsh
In inculcating the heritage of my glorious past
Their wish to fulfill their dreams
Which in their mind lasts
Sometimes the words of encouragement
Seems to be bewildering
At times a small little word is all for my healing

They share the strongest bond with me in grief
And biggest heart when happiness steeps my life

Even if they retire from their Earthly journey
The bond shall remain immortal
For parents are parents
Who will live on and on in me

Papa

My face glows the same as yours
My veins are as red as yours
Its flow is gentle though sometimes coarse
Holding your fingers tight and short
I walked with you and ran about
You recited verses from the Holy Quran
Every morning chilly or warm
Seeing me, peep through the slit of the cloth
You tickled and gave me a hot bath

In hurry and fury, you rushed for work
When hardly anyone even woke up
Even in a hurry and busy hours
You shared with me cola and fruit jars
My face gushed with happiness alas
When you picked me up from the class
Every gesture is vivid and clear
Of you waving from the two-wheeler

Indeed, time flew very fast
You disappeared into my past
Days were bitter and harsh for us
But second 'you' supported us
Tears always roll down my cheeks
To meet you once, hug and kiss
You will be you.... PAPA

Mummy

Mummy, the word which signifies
The unconditional love of the wise
Her delicate hands and fair face
In my heart has been traced
Her innocent and lovely smile
Made me feel, how special I mean
In her warm and caring shadow
Like an angel did I grow
Her presence made me free
Of the unbounded misery

One cursed night you left me alone
Along with the storm that came on
In this mist of loneliness and days so gloom
Your blooming love and care
Can never be replaced by someone else

I inherit your pure soul and spirit
Your kind nature do I possess
In successive years to be unfolded
I dream to become you more or less
May, the immortal soul be attired in a body again
And you keep living on in me forever

Golden Years
(Loreto Convent, Ranchi)

The day we entered the Loreto gate
With a neat uniform and a shiny face
We never cried and wept for long
For we had lovely teachers along
They sprinkled water on blooming buds
Who were planted with guts
We switched our brains to work
Memorizing theories and prose
As guiding lights, you strayed from heaven
In the form of learned women
The sapling grew into a plant
Some with flowers others with thorns
Imbibing the principles of Ward
By the sisters till the last

In this garden we also made friends
Hoping to reconnect now and then
Today, these years came to an end
Its time now to take blessings from thee
As these plants grow into a tree
May it give shelter once again t many
In this garden of pride and dreams

Discovering Life

Life seems to be cheerful and good
When you learn to enjoy it full
Where happiness has no limits
Unless you let the darkness hit
Your day remains only yours
Till your grin fascinates all
To mirth and the inevitable call

When you decide willingly
With passion and humble glee
Then the joyous world becomes your oyster
And friends your precious pearl

God bestows me with a gift each day
By linking me with lovely souls so gay
When you begin to discover them
No longer does life demarcate its boundaries to hell
Rather opens the door to a new castle

Lost in the house of my dreams
Amidst the frozen valley, & pines aligned
Carving memories on the fresh snow
With the loved ones jolly, and in full glow.

Vibrant Green

Leaves are the same, yet different
Color is the same yet more vibrant
Clouds enclose it in an oyster
Roots blow life to stems so faster

The trunk stands erect with a girth so wide
Bark encircles it like a life-guide
Branches circuits through the bush
Withholding buds, flowers, and fruits

Birds chirp inside their dens
In the nest with young ones to be fed
Tall trees kiss the sky
And brings showers of relief and sigh

Sun and rain nourish the leaflets
Flower blooms and fruits ripen
Whether spring's bloom or autumn's fall
The tree stands erect to withstand all

Blooming Buds

Every bud blooms one day
Be it today or some other fine day

When a bud transforms into a flower
It blooms all day and night long
Spreading fragrance in the air
Proclaiming to everyone its really worth all fair
These blooming hours last quite long
Enough for excelling in the lawn
Each eye willingly witnesses the beauty
Without failing to exhale its smell-fruity

Gradually the flower wilts away
Leaving behind petals all dry
The impression lasts forever in the soil
Sweeping through the new bluebells
Once again, the bud blooms
Be it today or some other fine day

Face of the Man

Although in this huge world
Full of pessimistic and optimistic aid
Man lies with his dear companions
Irrespective of their shallow or praiseworthy fate
He longs to live in their sweet presence
And performs his duty in its very essence

In the dramatic friend's role
Man for the sake of the other is but alone
He has to face the reward, good or bad
Of his deeds overall
Lord, never fails to reward the good and bad
For their cruel or good disposition in manhood

Sweet and Sour Years

Students' life brings bountiful joy
To every bug in some way

Studious bug spends all their time
In either mugging theories or straightening spines
They shut the windows of their thoughts
And spend lives in weights and blocks

Come discover life's true goal
Apart from studying in a single hole
They learn to cherish each moment
Apart from the book's burden huge
Some paint their canvas bright
Some hear music every night
Some transform their thoughts into lines
While others hoot with friends the whole night

Few get victimized by their mates
And wander in their land of dreams
These sweet-sour moments of our life
Remains fresh forever in our minds
It sweeps us each time
Into those glorious years of pride

Whitish Black

Life isn't enough to sigh at grief
It lacks space for someone meek
It portrays the two sides of heaven and hell
The darker side brings misery and compels us to yell
Casting over the pride of fellow
Inspiring her to grow in the moon's shadow

Every minute passes as a decade
In the darkness of the Earth's darker side
Once again Sun will rise from the East
Streaks of light fill her feast

Earth changed its side to mirth
Rising her limits beyond the bond

You are the Wind Beneath My Wings

You dwell in my heart's sweetest core
Guarding my flow to an awesome soul
When I peep through the blanket of time
You made me grow each day each night

Your kind gesture and selfless workout
Dwindled the pain and glorified the thought

Understanding and knowing your role
Enriched my experience of the human soul
Joyous memories owe only to you
Makes me smile and cry, that's true

Aspirations of Mankind

Man of courage, a man of understanding
With an open mind and lovely bonding
To cure and to be pure is its motto for all
With creative and deserving acting

Carrying responsibilities on its tender shoulders
Fighting as a martyr with countless boulders
To win for the nation and pious motherland
Strengthened everyone from the forthcoming struggle
Man of conscience and desires
Never lets down the hopes of thousands

Unknown to aggression, pinned to aspiration
Man of success endures for long
Creates harmony among all

Paths lead us to the new destination
Not knowing what awaits in the next
station
Beautiful scenery and a heartfelt journey
Leads us to a heavenly medley.

Head Towards Eternity

The unusual excitement and joy
Swept me in the land of your dreams
Your smile and passionate faith
Each time makes me feel you are there

Your trustful noteworthy presence
Fills my life with joyous essence
Your departure fills my heart with tears
Making me weep copiously over the years
Still, the hope lingers in my heart
That one day we move hand in hand

Your caring rash attitudes
Encircles me in clouds of gratitude
Your sweetness charms me a lot
Makes me feel shy, I doubt
This stage of our friendship
May gift us happiness and flips
To the better side of the heavenly trip

Taking vows to be together
In times of sorrow and laughter forever

Winter Has Gone

Waking up in the chilly morn
Taking milk with delicious corn
Sheep were gathering in the flock
Birds were chirping on the clock
The wondrous time of spring has come
With yellow flowers and songs to sing

First Summer Morning

One summer morning
When the sun was burning
Flowers were blooming
Shepherds were chatting
Pigeons cooed in the open air
Everything seemed so good and fair

Heights of Mockery

Every act can be limitless
Yet every act must have limits
Its core is never taught to the wise
As they imbibed it without cries
Merely, it's the tool of fools
Who abuse others by gathering pools
They are the dirt in the society
Who takes advantage of every faculty

The wise must disclose their wit
By getting rid of their useless trick
Sarcasm and dominance are their way
In reality, such fools have no friends
Fake challenges are of no help
In witnessing the truth unkept

Few seem not to change
And few who have the power to change the world
Like a river, the flow of life never stops
And these pebbles will someday drown
Every time it leaves a lasting impression
In my heart bountiful as an ocean's bed

London Kingdom

Once I went to London
To meet Mr. Pendum
I heard him say
Please look at my kingdom
My kingdom is so white
My kingdom is so red
My kingdom is so white and red
You please take right
I met his wife
His wife asked us to take left
There I met some thefts
I heard him say
Let's ruin them

Friends

You heal my wounds, not by herbs
Rather with words which itself heals
Broken heart and clouds of gloom
Never leaves a chance to bloom
Your presence makes me strong
Gives me the confidence to keep from wrong

You made me realize the gift of a smile
For that's free and full of life
As a helping hand, you stood always
And helped me with whatever you could
We didn't know each other for long
Days yet taught me a lot
When I rejoiced, you rejoiced with me
And when I cried you consoled me too
Your company surrounded me with laughter
Enlightened my brains grey matter

Your extended hand I held strong
For you are the essence of days so long
As a chain that always balances
Roses with thorns, days with the nights
And dramatic dreams with rash realty

Life

Every day passes by, but very few hardly realize
The real worth of the gifted life
Life is a verdict from the court of Nature
Whose witness is the future
Life is a mirror
Which reflects every error

Dreamland: Love

The excitement and joy
Crosses the bars of the sky
The soul is lightened all alone
By the flash of an unknown soul

Laymen describe them in words
Mocked and laughed at by the World
Except the two
No one realizes the serenity of that role

Often the heart's bell rings
And the circumstances sing
The song of two birds
Twittering around in the world of herds
Which never failed to victimize thousands
With very few holding hands till the end

A few spots are landmarks of inner peace
It wipes tears, sorrows, and pain away

Splendid King

Once there was a busy king
Who possessed a diamond ring
And married to a queen who sings

There was something that crackled
He had to go to wars and battle
Posing a sword of tough metal

When he fought upon his worries
He shouted at his army
And then solved things in a mess

Exam Fever

The student's reward for work and labor
Is not judged by marks on paper

Some work hard each day and night
Others fetch marks by studying the whole night
Some eat the fruits of their labor
Few chew the taste of failure
Which is just a ditch on a highway
Through which, their vehicle has lost its way

Now and then the vehicle accelerates
And makes its way with a new changed rate
Parents and teachers are the catalysts
Who boosts our confidence
Through encouragement and guidance

Those who earned their hard work
Must not flutter around as birds
Rather plan to raise the bars of race
Which new faces will be tempted to trace
And one bright day
Each face shall become a part of the race

Race

Seldom do we realize life is a race
Constantly enduring the never-ending chase
Paths remain diverged, and roads all blocked
Springing new ways of the old lot
Roots spread wide and branch diverse

Chirping birds and blooming buds
Spreading the aroma of nature's worth
Grasses sway and dance all-day
With yellow flowers all gay
A cool breeze with a soothing warmth
Evokes new life in every thorn

A platter of drops touches the canopy
Shouting its worth melodiously
He looks through the world of his prism
Showering colors into an even spectrum
Dusk overshadows the crowd
With stars twinkling above the ground

Smiling moon with a pale face
Peeping through a cloudy lace
The rising Sun greets us again
Pouring love, newness, and fun
Transformation and an excellent balance
Shapes the destiny of nature's efflorescence

Seldom do we realize life is a race
Constantly enduring the never-ending chase

Aid to a Prick

The prick of a pin just sucks a drop
But hatred for a person pricks the whole life
The evil remains to be evil
Making the surrounding a hard gravel
Who in turn loses hope and heart
Towards the most untrusted taunt

Our fate remains in the almighty's hand
Who has plans for both good and bad
When a pious soul is threatened by evil
Ancestors expressed that numerous doors open
Often the door continues to shut
And jerks us without any hope

The conscience awakes each time in me
With all-new zeal, vigor, and dream
My battle against evil and hopelessness
Every time crosses the streams too deep

God's Grace

The garden of love is the greatest of all
Which gives shelter to those who recall
The kind love and care of the Lord
It has the Yew trees of Borrowdale
Proclaiming to us the curse of Oblivion's
Love is so strong
That its bond is ever heartful

Love can bring us happiness from sorrow
And may melt a stone tomorrow
Love is an eternal bliss
Which dwells as a wish
Love never puts others down
Rather stays on the ground
It doesn't among them
But rather makes them one

Some take love for granted
While some remain deprived of love granted
Love is the cause of victory's good
And also the cause of someone's end too

Tiwari

You are the sun-kissed shadow of your mom
Growing every second as a storm
The glow on the cheeks symbolizes love
Whose life you have filled with love

Wet brown waves in your hair
When unfolded, loops into a velvety flow fair
Fanning lashes of your beady orbits
Adds extra pleasure to witty delights
Slim-hipped beauty with a playful smirk
Always ready for fabulous shots rock
Gentle, beautiful, and often obsessed
With scars, cuts, and the ego's bruised
All bones, yet so strong
To hold back tides that go wrong

Life still has sides to roll
Just wait and cherish those gone old
Destiny, desire, and dedication
Will someday catch hold of the collars of your ambition

One Spirit One Colour

The rainbow-hued in the freedom's new dawn
Encompassing the message of peace and pomp
Faces were cheerful and glad
As India hailed its independence flag
Under the shade of strong will and determination
The nation got freedom from whites
Created hatred among Indians and fight

The jubilance of peace spread in every corner
Rejoicing in one spirit and color
Children cheered in the fresh air
Carrying fragrance of truth and care

Words

Words are sword, which bleeds out loud
Unaddressed rage, locked in an emotional cage
Words are feathers, tickling the soul
Pouring happiness and reaching new goals

Words are metaphors, with the scent of joy and curse
The curve moves up and then down
With the articulation of each wound's sound

Power to build and shatter
Words always matter

Forever smiling and laborious
Sparkling softly on all bright occasions

Inside Out

Draped in the same skin
With variant colors and kin
Shouting with ever-increasing rage
And laughter strikes but fake

Ugly masks of melancholy
Gathers the maximum glee
The inner beauty hides, in the tears and evil grin wide
And the boat keeps sailing through all ports
With a tiny atomy of perks and hit jolts

Still to turn pages all new
Bundle of true emotions a few
Heart still recognizes only the truth
With arms clung over time's diverse root

Nature

Beads are pale but elegant too
Oysters are their abode, so true
Sea is salty yet so cool
Rising and falling in a loop
Nights are dark with constellations full
Nightingale enchants the verses full

Days were warm and breezy
A burning sun by the scanty pool
A platter of drops soothes our mind
Childish chatter outbursts aloud
Rustling dry leaves on the ground
Tickles down our nerve roots
Bushy tail hops and climbs
Rowing up and down the trees

Shadows chase us lifelong
Like naïve, we still catch along

Lap of nature is ever infinite
With ample flowers, fruits, and treats
It blooms and preserves so well.

My Oyster

I wish there was another day
Another moment, another new ray
I wish we made one more trip
Gossiping, dancing in the ribbed
Walking together and planning paces
Is only for fun and craziness
Smiling heartily and sleeping cozily
Taking care of each inch merrily
Be it storm, rain, or sun
Holding on and throughout bright

Habituating on either end of the core
Covering distances to bare each glow
Tales of lands, cultures, and borders
To neverending munching strands
Raindrops in the blue one, fitting under a single umbrella
for fun
Chilling over soft greens
Sipping tea and lemon delight
Sneaking each other boxes wrapped
And never wasting seconds reading and writing

Shouting and crying for reasons a hundred
Consoling and listening to the dead
A few pages are all luck
Plucking fruits from destiny and time

The best moments take time,
And we lived it in no time
Exploding joy and laughter
I miss myself without my OYSTER.

Never Stop

The rising sun and a new day
Brings us hopes of a warm ray
Stop hiding worries behind your grin
Smile both from in and within

We can teach our minds to mind
A day never comes where things are inline
Yet, we are supposed to be fine

The zeal and determination will always stand tall
Ignorant of neverending worries and falls
Work as if no day is left
Stop overthinking the results yet.

Emptiness

The day is so good, new, and, precious
So long we cheer and sing songs melodious
Not even a second is promised as planned

The volume of junk our brain handles,
Can easily fill rooms of disgrace and puddles.
That matter occupies our box so grey,
Yet fails to build us intelligent and gay.

As we roll with each passage of time,
Those junks were not meant to be rented in.
The only thing conclusive remains our MIND,
Soundly sheltering hopes, patience and love aligned.
Through roads of loss, betrayal, despair, guilt ill-timed.

Time changes but MIND needs to be changed.
To equate happiness, sorrows, regrets, and goodness.
Programing our MIND is a tricky task,
Whose password is acceptance unmasked

Time

Trapped within the traces of time
With uniform ticks and circular rhyme
Endless specks, people, and plans
Keeps flipping and skidding in chains

Leaping is not our way
Neither do they favor shorter rays
Tick and step counts us bucks
Manages sorrows, smiles, and luck
No phase lasts more than a second
Revolving happiness, rewards, and lessons

Taking each step in order so wise
Life never stumbles anticlockwise
It gears each time when charge knocks
Making it still, silent all blocked
We run with it on and off
Bearing in mind that it will not pause
Can there be a better present
In pacing work and freezing moments

Synchronizing in bits the mechanical complex
Letting it run smoothly as a helix
The whole world is stacked in TIME
As an umbrella holding LIFE

The Storm

I wish there was a fine day
Gleeful and careless as I sway
I wish you fed me with your hands
And chose the best one for me last time
I wish I could nag as a baby
And gobble treats of choco and candy
I wish I could lie on your extended arm
Singing out loud whatever I want
I wish there was no such storm
Neither was our small world blown

I wish you knew how much I crave
For your touch on my forehead
I wish you know how I bear
Reach and every particle you left
You turned me into a sweet bud
An epitome of strength and self-worth
I gave all to heal and console
And did justice to my conscience right

I light so many lives you left
My inner spark remains unlit
Exploring new places, people, and things
Still pushes way to void within
I do sob and weep all alone
Finding out reasons to fill my full
You are the magician to my life's miracles
The unexpected happiness and guilty pleasures

I wish we rejoice again one day
Escaping from these dramatic good days

I know that you know all
Even before I acknowledged this call
I know that your plans are the BEST
No matter how much I roll.

Stretching Ends

In the sober stillness of this night
I miss my real happy soul
In the calm and peaceful time
I fight with the anxious tides within
In the happy glorious world
I find no one to rely on
In this judgmental crowd
I fail to truly laugh loud

Around my loved ones
I still feel lost and abandoned
At the end, everyone truly has a family
Ready to take sides and correct lies
I still wait for the ones whom I used to call family

Tired enough of pulling up relations
Hiding mistakes and unnecessarily finding good reasons
Tired of patching families and faking a smile
Tired of saying yes.... To all the petty things
Because the world has portrayed me as a young sufferer
of LIFE
And others as a protector of time.
Time flew and it gifted more than enough
But in this stillness of the night, I stand all alone
Fearful of losing all I could hold in my small fist

Infinite Crystals

Can we touch the sky?
And keep calm and light
Can we dive into the rainbow?
Emerging all colorful and vibrant
Can we pluck stars from the dark sky?
And keep shining all night
Can we drench in heavy rain?
Washing our dirt now and then
Can we ripple endlessly like a river?
Carrying and soaking our deeds over

Do we miss basking in the sun?
Making us crisp as a baked bun
Oh, you wind to carry me within
To places new, happy and dim

We can bloom wherever we want
Into lavender, petunia, or a thorn
The right soil, water, sand, sun
Is always available in tons
We need to learn to rise again
And build ourselves a new DEN

My Fair Lady

I wish I could have grown
And have known you little more
I wish I never nagged and cried
I wish to have cuddled you hard
To hear beats that no longer beep
I wish I could eat one more platter
And never felt hungry anymore
I wish to have argued with you
And to realize that I wasn't true
I wish to be a little more stubborn
And to know what happened to you MOM

I hope to care just as you
And match your taste as you do

I wish you here so strong
For I never had to gulp tears alone
Wish to imbibe your virtues
Apart from beauty surpassing along
Waiting patiently for nature to transcend its gear
And help me be your fruitful heir

Circle

We chase our happiness and demise
Or we cultivate rage and kindness
We overthink beyond the box
And keep dwindling our mind's clock
Do we cherish the day's light
And admire the charm of the night
We cheer and laugh out loud
And fail to let our hearts shout

Anguish, arrogance, and rage creep at a quicker pace
We built our egos so thick, failing to reconnect with it
We still search for rosy cheeks or mass over the ribs
Could we just live as we wish, ignoring what others think

Let's live in the present as gifted
And take not things for granted
LIFE is a forever storm
Restoring and restarting for all

Freshness brings happiness
Calmness mimics smoothness
Disasters remind me of Rage
Transformation hooks newness

Drizzling

Winding up the heavy trolley
With glaring looks all folley
Smiling with a sweet smirk
Pushing through the tiny burps
Hair rolling down the blades
Of shoulder, bouncing forth ahead

Short stature with small steps
Super fast cadence and wide stretch
Lack of curvature, full of life
Always proved a valid spine
Thin and tender fingers glow
The collar beauty we all adore
Mandibular prominence which you inherited
Reminds of your mother's presence.
Stepping through each lane alone,
Created a warrior lifelong
Keeping away from Show and pomp
Craving for a second living bond

A kind observer and a silent joker
Very considerate and peacemaker
Being happy and keeping promises
Expressing a lot to a few bosses

The life you live revolves around few
Be it family or friends true
Keeping pace with life's plan
Ponder of expanding your clan

Flowers wilt and ashes blow
We all shall one day rise and go
Accomplish every bit you desire
With mental peace and hard work as a fire
Emotions often sweep us to the shore
Keep yourself in the core

Life is eternal and the soul immortal
The body perishes all in total
We can't hold time and persons in our life
Those needed will rewind
Destiny has lovely chapters
Ringing the door when it matters
Live, laugh, and explore more
Who knows, when we last snore

Chores of Mind

Some smile even when frustrated
Few laugh even when dejected
Many are kind even after hatred
Few are lovable even when rejected
A lot of us are curious about achieving success
Knowing very well that we cannot rush access
Plans fall in pits right there
Devoid of worries, tension, and despair
With all will and dedication
No one curious misses any station
In this sweet-sour journey of LIFE
Let's forever smile, love, laugh, and be kind

Speak

Words can engulf us
In the ocean of emotions
Words can deviate us
When overpraised in excess
Words can bring tears
If said harshly and in anger
Words leave us happily satisfied
When we speak by chance wise
Words do heal at times
If right exclamations were insight
Words reflect the inner voice
Especially in anger, hatred, and fight
The impact lasts for so long
Forcing us to know what's wrong
Words signify our true nature
Being rational and soft always prosper
Pledging to speak all true, soft, and solemn
Echoing the ambiance and present situation

Thunder

Breathing fresh facing the sea
Relieves miseries and worries too many
Lane of trees on either side
Branching to the top as the ceiling is so wide
Crooked benches, swinging aside the roads
Golden Bamboo turned into comfy boats
Far and far roars the wind
All at once thundering begins
Pouring drops and harsh gust
Swept the tides of water like dust
Darker clouds danced fiercely
Escaping from this trap was not easy
Experiencing the sudden unexpected weather
Holding tight and feeling the jitter
Alas! finding the way out
Hoping for this to once pause
Joyous at heart, and a little scared
Still, a victory to have survived...

Calm Mind

Can we pace our thoughts for good?
Can we manifest only what we should?
Can we embrace the truth as it is?
Can we ever not bother with others' shit
Can a human live in peace?
Can we not be biased in greed?
Can we imagine what purpose we serve?
Can we pause and rewind to work?
Can we poke our nose into our work?
Can we use a little mind at research?
Can we try to be good and kind?
Can we survive with all our rights?
Can we still talk without arguing?
Can we not understand without shouting?
Oh! All seems a tricky misnomer
Rather human multiple personalities isomers
Time, situation, and the pain
Never heals as per plan.

Dadda (Grandmom)

My first go-to person succeeding Mom
Was a very kindhearted sweet grandmom
Looking into her sparkling brown eyes
Comforted me all the time
Sober, calm, and ever ready to serve
Was her daily behavior since birth
Busy with the daily small chores
And barely cared about what she wore

My best fond memories with her were at night
When I tucked myself into her so tight
She would then pat me to sleep
Reciting verses from the Quran and Hadith
The tasty meals and endless care
Devotion to pray and never to talk in rage
Her fragile touch, calmness, bare wish
And warm hug I always cherish

Life never goes our way
For His plans are different, they say
In a night's flip, she left
Too early for a new life after death
She lives in me as a soft-hearted woman
A very caring and overprotective human
My granny was one best person
Blessing me in every situation.

Dada (Grandfather)

The dark tone frowned face
Acting rationally devoid of race
Never demanding materialistic things
Satisfied in minimal clings
Man of people and great talks
Gregarious in nature and logic that rocked

Very stern and wise at words
Be it Urdu, English, or Arabic quotes
History lover of the wide world
Firm in Islam and woods
Walked head to head with plans
Firm advisor and manager in the town
Straightforward, joyous, and an able believer
Passionate for greenery, croutons, and climbers
Loved an honest sustainable life
Tried very best to be a noble guide

Education was his wings of gold
Imparted to others and helped them mold
Never gave up in harsh time
Build up spirits to bear fine
Neither stored grudges but chose to spoke
Irrespective of whomsoever known
Grateful man who build a home
Made of love bricks with his beloved

He is the root of our thoughts
To our work, academics, or job
A respectful person full of dedication
Even in cooking meals for his grandchildren
He taught us verses from the holy Quran
Discussed endlessly the heritage of past
Curiously delivered all that he knew
Always wanted books a few
He grew roses, marigolds, and jasmine
Kept us away from negativity and evil

His tales of building mosques and libraries
Encouraged us to join in the glory
The best orator and sweet observer on the lawn
Slept early and woke up before dawn
My fond memories of reading out to him
From newspapers and trophies, I used to win
Narrating him in excitement all my stories
Of the people, books, and new cities
Watching with him Mughleazam all chrome
Awestruck by his expressions of shock

He groomed plants and my mind
Taught me to fly against the wind
Food was his savior till last
Enabled us to try hands-on recipes fast
Cared and always guarded me
Since a child where I bicycled
No matter what others do
Was so just, I must tell you
He suffered yet could smile
Faithfully performed his duties till the last tide

The best chapter in gold
Is my DADA till age fine old
Resides in the vibes of my home
Lives in the leaves and good hopes
His blessings and prayers will thrive
For me and my family alike
The perfect example of God's creation
And a part of all my bright notions

Take one step at a time
Hold on to Life
Think with your brain
Dance with your feet

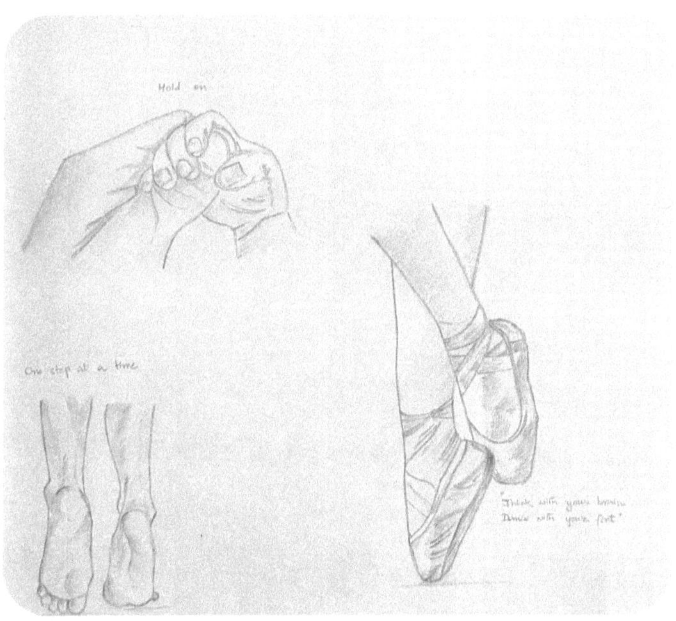

www.ingramcontent.com/pod-product-compliance
Lightning Source LLC
Chambersburg PA
CBHW022104150726

47990CB00003B/1247